"A"
DIFFERENT
KIND OF
SUPERPOWER

∞

Bradley Riches & James A Lyons

Welcome

Hi, I'm Bradley Riches and I have a superpower. Yes, you read that right! But I don't have superhuman strength and I can't turn invisible. I have a different kind of superpower. I am autistic. To me, that is even better.

My parents told me that I was autistic a long time ago now. I remember that day as clearly as if it were yesterday. Why? Because it's an important part of my life, and it helped me become who I am today. So, please, let me tell you a story. Let me fill

you in on the details of me and my superpower.
Let me take you on a journey that's very special to
me and has been since I was nine years old.

∞

Think about this for a moment: how would you feel
if one day your parents came into your room and
told you that you had a superpower?

Excited? Definitely.

Powerful? Maybe.

The world is full of extraordinary people, but
some have unique abilities that set them apart from
everybody else. You might know these gifts as
superpowers.

Now, what do we know about superpowers?

From watching films, you might now be
thinking about superhuman strength or the ability
to communicate with animals.

Perhaps it might be the ability to race
through the sky at incredible speeds, flying high
above the ground on your way to save people from
dangerous situations.

The thing is, I am not talking about those

types of superpowers; I am talking about actual superpowers. *Real* superpowers. Superpowers that exist in everyday people like you. You all have one. I do too. In fact, we should all be wearing capes right now.

I believe that having a superpower can be an electrifying and energising experience, and one that and is also unique to each person. With a superpower, you might feel more confident (like being brave enough to read out loud in the classroom). You might feel more capable of achieving the seemingly impossible. At the same time, having a superpower also comes with a great deal of responsibility (as famous superheroes are often told). When having a special gift, you need to consider the consequences of using your new powers.

Firstly, I'd like to ask you this: Would you want a superpower?

You said yes, didn't you?

Why wouldn't you?

Okay, secondly: What superpower do you

want?

Have you chosen? Yes? Good.

I am going to attempt to mind read now (though mind reading isn't actually my superpower!). I think you chose the ability to fly, invisibility, or maybe you chose having the power to control the weather. Am I along the right lines?

When I was younger, I would have probably picked the same as you. These are like the powers that I mentioned earlier... the ones you have seen in films whilst you picked away at your popcorn.

The reality is that superpowers can be much more wide ranging. *Real* superpowers are even more special than being able to fly or climb buildings or teleport yourself to different countries in a matter of seconds.

You may be wondering why I am telling you all of this. Well, as you know, I am lucky enough to have a very definite superpower. A real one! But how did I feel when I first found out? I wasn't excited. I was actually confused.

Though, overtime I learnt that it is okay to feel confused. It is okay to take some time to figure out who you are and work out how all the parts of your personality fit together to show the big, beautiful product at the end.

I have figured things out now and I wouldn't change who I am for anyone. It took me some time, and there were ups and downs, but I got there in the end. That's all that matters.

Let's think about a giant Lego set. I love Lego. Every single human is like a Lego set. Why? Because each block represents a different part of us, and each part comes together to make the whole product. This is just like how there are so many elements that go together to build a human!

The building blocks you get when you first open the colourful Lego box may not look like much on their own, but every single piece, regardless of its shape or colour, contributes to the overall product.

What I mean is: you wouldn't be you without all the little parts that add up together.

My favourite ever Lego set was the Lego City Airport. I got this as a present for my eighth birthday, and as soon as I had torn off the blue and yellow wrapping paper, I had to start building it immediately. There were seven hundred and three building blocks in this set. From them, I built a communications tower, an aeroplane, a terminal, and then a few smaller things, like a luggage lorry. Some parts were easy, but other parts were a little trickier to put together. The little yellow people fit together quickly, so I soon had a pilot, a person who guided the planes in, and a little man in a Hawaiian shirt, holding a brown suitcase in his hand.

What I am trying to say is, these small additions may not seem important at first but are needed to make the set whole.

Once I had the little people ready, I built the control tower and the terminal with its big glass windows. After that, I just had the large plane to build. The plane was white with a big red tail. Building this plane is what working out who you are is like. You have all the pieces, they all seem to blend into each other, and it takes time to figure out where each part belongs.

You have to focus on spending time finding the little, black blocks that make up the plane steps. The instructions say there are six, but you only find five after the first look through the pile. There is no shame in taking as much time as you need to find every part that is needed to complete the set, in the same way that there is no time limit to figure out just who you are. There is no rush to put all the pieces together.

Slowly though, every part of your Lego personality is put into the correct place. You can sit back, feeling content with having everything worked out. However, occasionally, something may come along and shake the structure you tried so hard to build (like my sister Emily accidentally kicking the baggage lorry across the room!). When this happens, you then have to spend even more time putting the pieces back to where they belong. This is okay, though. As long as you have all the pieces, everything will work out fine.

You can also ask people to help you pick up the knocked over Lego so you can rebuild it. This is okay as well. We are not designed to figure things out on our own all the time.

When the set is finally complete, the more you look at it, the more the little details stand out. The green rubbish bins. The small computer. The little blue parking sign. Every part of the build is significant. Just like every part of you is significant.

∞

Now, before I go on any further, let me properly introduce myself. My name is part of my Lego set, just like yours is too, so let's start there...

My full name is Bradley Stephen Riches, and I am currently talking to you from the stairs in my childhood home. By the way, I would like to say that my middle name is always Stephen with a *p* and a *h*, not a *v*. My surname is *Riches*... the word 'rich' *plus* 'es'. Not Richards or Richardson. I say this because the number of times that I was at school and have been called by the wrong name is probably too high to count! Has that ever happened to you?

I was born on the eleventh of December 2001. This makes me a Sagittarius (The Archer). I was born at precisely eleven o'clock in the morning. I love this fact because eleven is my favourite number.

On the days when I check my phone or see a clock that says 11:11am, I make a wish. A fun fact about my birthday is... I was born on this day! I'm just kidding, that's an obvious fact! On the same date (but years before my birth!), the crew for the final Apollo mission landed on the moon, which is awesome!

I'd love to travel to space and see all the colourful planets and twinkling stars up close. Also, my birthday is exactly two weeks before Christmas Day and it is the 345th day of the year, if it isn't a leap year, of course. What else might be important to know about me? Well, my favourite film is *The Incredibles*, and I love making homemade lemonade with my mum (it's my favourite drink!).

What's a fun fact about you?

The Beginning

I am now sitting at the table in my kitchen, with a drink and a plate of snacks beside me. I have brought you in here to rewind a bit, and answer the burning question:

How did all of this superpower thing start?

Well, I'm taking you on a journey and telling you the story of how I discovered my special superpower.

Let's start off with where I am sitting at the moment...

The kitchen is an odd room. So much

happens in the kitchen of any house. Every Christmas meal comes out of this room. The dining table is the centre of both difficult and happy conversations. It is the place where you can break exciting news or catch up with your family and friends. It's also where you can get the latest family gossip over dinner!

I remember sitting around this table whilst my family sang '*Happy Birthday*' to me every single year. The rectangular table here used to have a white tablecloth with circles of all different colours on it. I can remember it so clearly, but now it has been replaced with a blue one.

I used to prop my dad's camera up on this table and film myself singing musical songs as I stood in the kitchen. I'd move the fruit bowl to the edge of the table and lean the camera against it. Looking back now, I never got a perfect angle!

Most importantly, this table is where I first heard about my superpower. I wasn't told exactly what it was, but I found out I had one.

It was on the eighteenth of September 2010,

and I had just finished my breakfast. Both my parents entered from the hallway. They sat down next to me.

"Bradley, we need to let you know that you have a superpower," my dad said, kindly.

I stared back at them both blankly. "A real superpower? What is it?"

What I didn't know at the time was that the doctor had phoned them up that morning to tell them the news. The doctor had explained that I had a different kind of superpower, not the type that I had seen in films before.

After being told this, I sat confused for a little while. Dad brought me a glass of lemonade, and I sipped it. I wasn't quite sure what my superpower was yet, my parents hadn't told me. But I didn't feel like I had a superpower.

Mum smiled at me then turned to dash out of the room. "Wait here a minute, Bradley!" she shouted, excitedly, over her shoulder as she hurried away, towards the staircase.

She returned a few minutes later, carrying a

big bucket.

"Here you go," she said, putting it down in front of me and giving me a big smile. It was a simple, plain, blue bucket. Dad or Mum had done a bit of craftwork, as there were letters stuck to the outside. I picked it up and spun it around in my hands so I could see what it said:

SUPERPOWER OF THE DAY.

When I read these words, my confusion was overtaken by excitement. I wanted to know what its purpose would be.

"Have a look inside," Mum said, whilst taking hold of my hand. "Just make sure you don't drop the contents everywhere."

I tilted the bucket and poked my head over the top. I stared down at a pile of neatly folded bits of paper. I wasn't sure how many there were, but I counted at least twenty. "What are they?" I asked.

Dad came and sat down next to me. "Each one of those pieces of paper has a different superpower written on it."

I was impressed. My parents had obviously

taken a lot of time to write a list of all the superpowers that they could think of and then added each one separately into the bucket.

"One of them is very special," said Mum.

I looked up as she spoke. "How is it special?" I asked.

"You see, one of those pieces of paper has your real superpower on it."

"Which one?" I asked.

"You'll have to wait and find out, Bradley," Dad said, mysteriously. He waved his hands in the air, and I giggled. "One day your real power will be revealed to you."

Little did I know at the time, the day that I was to find out my superpower would be so special. Let me tell you this: it is so tempting when you are under ten years old to just grab all the slips of coloured paper and read them in excitement.

With the bucket, there was one main rule: I was only allowed to choose one piece of paper at a time, and this could only be done on days when Mum or Dad told me so.

I was disappointed, but I understood. I was to experience different superpowers over the next couple of months, until I could find out my real superpower.

"Don't worry, Bradley," Mum grinned. "When you find out your real superpower, it will all make sense."

Always Unique

DING DING DING

That was my alarm clock. I woke up at exactly 8:11am, just like I did every single day. It was a Saturday in 2010. This was when I was first allowed to pick a slip of paper out of the bucket, and I couldn't contain my excitement.

I jumped out of my bed and headed to the bathroom ready to have my morning shower. Before I was to find out my superpower, I had to get ready for the day.

I crept into the hallway. Mum was still asleep in bed. My mum was the only one who knew how to make the water in the shower the perfect temperature for me. You see, the shower has two dials that you need to turn in order to make it work. Whenever I tried to do it myself, I never got it quite right.

Mum had shown me many times, so I knew that the right-hand dial needed to be positioned as if it was pointing to the number six on a clock. Then, the left-hand dial needed to be pointing to three o'clock.

I was determined to try to do it myself that day.

So, I reached into the shower and had a go; I pulled my arm back when it was hit by cold water. I was so close to getting it right myself, so I turned the nobs again. Despite being sure they were in the right spot, the water didn't feel right to me. I decided to wait until Mum woke up.

After a while of waiting, Mum sorted the shower for me as soon as she woke. She laughed as she walked across the landing, with me trailing just behind her.

"I haven't even had breakfast yet, Bradley!"

After washing my hair, I squirted the perfect amount of scented shower gel into my hand and got myself clean, before drying off and heading back to my bedroom.

The next step in my routine was to put my clothes on. Every evening, before I went to bed, I made sure that I laid out my clothes for the following morning. That way when I was washed, I could find them on top of the chair near my desk.

Boxer shorts, then trousers, then a t-shirt. I put them on and sat on my bed. After this, I grabbed my 'Saturday socks' from my top dresser drawer.

I ran the socks through my hands, just how I did every morning. I held them for a moment, feeling them to make sure that they were soft (just the way I liked them). I didn't understand why I got so upset about the way they felt, especially if the texture felt different to its usual touch. Fear not though, whenever I did get overwhelmed at textures, Mum always came to my rescue.

Let me tell you a little about her, as I don't know where I'd be without her.

My mum is called Susan and was born on the seventh day of December 1974. This also makes her a Sagittarius (The Archer). It's cool that we both have birthdays during the same week. On the day that she was born, a famous singer called Barry White was number one in the charts with a song called *'You're the first, the last, my everything'*. I tell you this because Mum used to hum along to it every time it came on the radio. Mum also loved to sing it when doing the housework, just like she was doing this Saturday!

After getting ready and making my way downstairs, I entered the living room to see Mum dusting the shelves filled with my school pictures and the photographs from the times I was in school plays.

I loved performing at school. I think being on stage gave me some of my favourite memories. I also enjoyed acting in the school nativity when I was in primary school. One year I was cast as a King, which was quite a fun part to play. Another year I was a star. Mum said she enjoyed every show I was in.

I caught Mum smiling down at the pictures as she cleaned them. She then took the vacuum cleaner in her hand and walked past me, ruffling my hair as she did so. She began sucking up the dirt from the wooden flooring in our hallway. She was cleaning the whole of the downstairs like she did every Saturday morning, and she was singing along to her music.

Then I thought: does my mum have a superpower as well?

Then I remember: everyone does!

But, what is hers?

Her superpower must be that she can solve anything. This is very true. My mum can literally solve *everything*. There was one time when I was about six or seven-years-old and I was walking barefoot around the house. I stood on a staple. I think it had fallen out of some of my dad's paperwork which had been left on the small side table. I hopped into the kitchen and sat down, shouting for my mum. At the time, I thought I was going to die because there was just so much blood coming out of my foot. To me it looked like a scene from a horror film!

As I sat on the chair, Mum came over and pulled the staple out before holding a tissue on the wound to stop it bleeding further. I remember exactly what my mum said to me as I was sitting there worrying.

Now, in this situation you might think that a mother would say something loving like: "Don't worry Bradley, it will all be okay." Not my mum. Her exact words were: "Stop being so dramatic!"

Close enough though, I guess, and she did mean well. My mum is so kind and loving to me, even if she is the one to tell me when I'm being overly dramatic.

Flash forward a few years, and there was another time where she solved something for me when I was faced with a difficult situation. I was out one evening with my whole family, and we were sitting in an Italian restaurant near the middle of town. I am not sure if we were there to celebrate something. Perhaps it was Emily's birthday? I can't quite remember. The waiter had come to our table with a plate of food for each of us. My sister began eating her lasagne straight away, but I just stared at my food. After a couple of minutes, my mum noticed.

"Come on Bradley, don't let it go cold," she had told me.

I looked up at her sadly. "There's green grass on my pizza. I can't eat anything green."

What I didn't know when I ordered this type of pizza, was that it came with green peppers and rocket on top!

Mum could have tried to make me eat it. She could have told me off and said that I had to eat the food I had been given. Before this moment, my mum didn't know that I couldn't eat anything green. I couldn't explain why, but she understood me.

When I told her about not wanting to eat the 'grass', she didn't tell me to stop being so dramatic again. No. This time she said, "don't worry Bradley, we can fix this. We can get you another pizza with no grass on it. Dad will happily eat this one for you!"

Little things like this meant, and still mean, so much to me. It is the little gestures that she does that help comfort me when I am upset or confused. It isn't always words, either. It could just be a hand on mine or a gentle rub of my forearm. After saying that I could choose something else to eat, I turned and smiled at her.

At the time, I was young and couldn't fully appreciate what she had done for me. But now, I know I am so thankful to have a mum like her. A mum who understands me. Once I was no longer upset, she gave me a hug around the waist and said that my superpower was a beautiful thing.

By this time, I knew what my superpower was, so I knew what she meant, and I believed her.

"Bradley, your superpower is a beautiful thing."

Throughout the years, I replayed these words in my head over and over to make sure I remembered them. It didn't stop my confusion sometimes, but overtime I learnt that this was normal.

I used to repeat it like a mantra, but would sometimes doubt myself and my power. If I ever said this aloud, Mum would put her hand on my arm and tell me:

"Bradley, you have always been unique, and that is what's beautiful."

After saying this, she would always hold me, like a big human comfort blanket, and kiss me on the forehead. We would sometimes stay in an embrace for a few minutes. Once Mum had made sure that I was okay, she would pour me a glass of homemade lemonade before leaving me to go and play with my imagination.

Now you know about my mum's superpower,

let me tell you about the first superpower I picked from the bucket.

I remember being nervous and excited at the same time. Dad brought the bucket down from the high shelf in the kitchen and placed it in front of me. He was beaming from ear to ear. He was just as excited as me!

ABILITY TO FREEZE

"What a funny superpower!" I laughed, but I was so excited to try this out.

For the rest of the day, Dad and Mum (and Emily, begrudgingly) had to stand as still as a statue whenever I shouted, "FREEZE!"

Gosh, it was fun. Looking back on this day, we had such a laugh. I told them to freeze every ten minutes!

Trying Different Superpowers

Let me tell you about my childhood bedroom now, and how it was such a safe space for me. When I was growing up, I spent a lot of time creating an environment that was perfect in making me feel happy and secure. The first thing you should know about my bedroom is that there was a heavy London theme throughout. I absolutely loved the idea of London whilst growing up.

You can't go one day without seeing something that reminds you of the capital city.

If you watch television today, I bet you will see imagery of London. It might be a character walking through central London, hailing a black taxi from outside a grand building. The character may jump out minutes later and enter a restaurant in Covent Garden or Soho, or maybe down one of the even more exclusive places in Mayfair.

Those restaurants always look so fancy. There are often big plants at the entrance, with doors opened by people dressed in posh, long maroon coats with black and gold hats on their heads.

Other television shows may show different parts of London, like Eastenders. Every news bulletin will have a story linked to something that has happened there too. If you are currently reading a British based book (like this one!), there is likely to be a mention of London somewhere.

We haven't even touched on movies yet either! Comedies, thrillers, horrors, period dramas, action, love stories: every genre will have a film that has been set in London. Think of your top ten films of all time. The chances are that one of them has a background of the Thames or giant glass skyscrapers at some point during it.

My favourite part of London is Big Ben.

Fun fact: its actual name is the Elizabeth Tower, and Big Ben is just the name of the bell that sits inside it. This is the bell that rings every new year, sending chimes of hope and positivity. The fact that it is actually the name of the bell doesn't matter though, if you say Big Ben to people, they will know exactly what you are talking about. You often get some who will try to correct you and say *"...well, actually that's just the name of the bell,"* but feel free to ignore them. You have my permission to do so.

Before I ever went there, London seemed like such a great place. The thoughts of red phone boxes and buses, clean buildings and a wide blue river made it a perfect theme to choose for my room. It made me feel at peace. I also like the Union Jack (another fun fact: it's actually called a Union Flag, and only a Union Jack if it is flown from a boat).

I did get to visit London eventually but was sadly left feeling overwhelmed. Nothing prepares you for how busy it is compared to your hometown, especially if you grew up in a quiet area like I did.

The noise from the traffic is loud, and you can taste the pollution from the exhaust fumes. People are everywhere, and they always are in a rush!

In fact, everything is noisier in London. The people bustle and jostle you, and you seem to spend the whole time trying to dodge pedestrians as if you're like a skier in the winter Olympics. The London Underground might be the worst part for this, made even worse by having to go through a lot of deep, narrow tunnels which seem impossible to escape.

When I went to London for the first time, I was taken to the big aquarium which sits near the London Eye. I think we may have had some of those vouchers that get you a two-for-one entry. You know, those ones you always see on the back of cereal boxes or on multipacks of crisps.

We entered through the giant entrance hall then moved onto the dark corridors. I wasn't sure what caused it, but it felt a bit suffocating at first, and the deeper that we got, the more it felt as if I was being trapped inside. I ran back towards the entrance and sat on the cold floor beside a tank that contained jellyfish.

I focused on the tank, and it seemed to calm my nerves. The water inside was a dark blue, and the lighting meant that the creatures appeared slightly neon. Above my head, seahorses swam around in a separate tank. Watching them swim peacefully around comforted me, and I stopped to stare at their movements for a long time. I wondered if they were safe, trapped inside their tank that couldn't have been more than six feet long.

Maybe if I had the superpower that allowed me to talk to animals I could tap on the glass and ask them. But that wasn't my superpower of the day. Also, I wouldn't know what the first question I'd ask them would be!

I stared at the creatures as they looped up and down in the water. Mum and Dad walked around, looking at the fish themselves, but I stayed there until I felt more prepared to venture further into the busy attraction. I knew they were happy to wait for me, as long as I was still in their eye-line.

The busyness of London made me feel like changing the theme of my room to another great city, like New York City. Time Square always looks so incredible on television, but it must also be extremely busy. There were also so many flashing lights, neon signs and odd noises there, so I knew it may also be overwhelming for me. I would still like to visit there someday though.

Every part of my bedroom's decorations were put together by me. It was always my safe space. There was usually soft music playing gently in the background, and I had hung rainbow-coloured lights around the edges of the ceiling. If I ever felt the need to truly switch off, I would often make small forts out of my bedsheets. They became a forcefield between me and the outside world.

Often when I was alone, I sat in one of my forts, confused with all the questions that my mind seemed to be asking me. So many thoughts would race through my head.

How long had they known I had a

superpower?

Had they always had superpowers too?

When did their parents tell them about their powers?

Were they born in a radioactive lab?

What if my dad had been bitten by a special insect when younger, and I hadn't been told?

Each time I went to bed he could be jumping between buildings in our town, saving people and becoming a hero in our community. I've never seen any superhero suits in the wash basket though, so maybe this is unlikely. But who knows?

Before I found it out, I would quite often try to work out what my real superpower was. I would search my brain, trying to figure out any special powers that I used without realising. But I could only think of the ones I had picked out of the bucket. And I knew they weren't real powers, not like the one my parents told me I had. By this time,

I had taken around five slips of paper from the bucket. I had pretended to be invisible. I used this to creep around and jump out on people when they weren't expecting it. My mum wasn't a fan of this superpower. When I jumped out on her she screamed: "Bradley, my tea! Be careful!"

It was a fun power to have briefly though, but I was glad that it wasn't my real superpower.

Another time I had flight. I had to get Dad to help with this. I was laid on top of the ironing board facing the television, watching a YouTube video taken from the cockpit of a plane. This made it feel like I was actually flying through the clouds. Dad borrowed my sister's hairdryer and had it on full blast on the cold setting so that I could feel the wind rushing through my hair.

"What can you see on the ground, Bradley?" Dad would ask every few minutes.

I would think and shout out things like "Buckingham Palace!" and "the Atlantic ocean!". I travelled the entire world that day.

The Superpower Bucket was so much fun to start with, but with each superpower I tried, I started to think more about which one I really possessed.

Am I like a strong man and able to smash down walls with my bare hands? Maybe. Maybe not. I told Dad I'd like to be strong. When I was younger, I punched a wall once when I couldn't control my emotions, but that hurt me more than it hurt the wall. I ended up with bruised knuckles!

Another thought I had was that I had super-speed. That was a fun morning when I was allowed to try that. I put on my newest trainers and attempted to run to the local Tesco Express and back in under thirty seconds. I only made it to the end of our road before I was out of breath, so super-speed wasn't my real power either.

A few times I wondered if my superpower was the ability to perform a double backflip whenever, and wherever, I wanted. I never got to try that. Dad said it wasn't in the bucket "because of health and safety concerns."

Even as I've gotten older, I still haven't tried a backflip. Bradley does not want to break his neck today, or any day, thank you very much!

Tremendously Intelligent

Anyway, back to the story of how I found everything out. What do we know? Well, I had a superpower, and I didn't know what it was. I had tried many other superpowers, but none felt quite right. I was still waiting for the day I'd find my true power.

This used to frustrate me so much that sometimes I wished I didn't have a superpower at all. If I said this, Dad used to tell me that even the bad superpowers that I didn't really enjoy having gave me the chance to express myself. If I didn't have my real superpower, I wouldn't be who I am today.

I definitely wanted a superpower if it was like one of those that I pulled from the bucket I was given. Even my least favourite powers allowed me to spend more time with my Dad.

Let me tell you a bit about him now.

My dad is called Colin; however, most people know him as Cols. I don't think we look alike, but everyone says we do. The main difference is that he has a bald head and not cool hair like me.

Dad was born on the sixth of November 1974, which makes him a Scorpio (The Scorpion). He first met my mum when they were much younger. They were childhood sweethearts, which I think is pretty cool!

Both of my parents have always had a love for cooking. They were cooking in the same room at school years and years ago and had been given a practical assignment which involved making some kind of pasta dish. I'm not sure exactly what it was, but most pasta dishes are the same, aren't they?

Well, they are to me anyway… but don't tell my dad I said that.

Anyway, my dad was finding it hard to perfect his pasta dish. Maybe he hadn't done his preparation homework (unlike me; I always used to do mine at school!). In class, my mum noticed that he was struggling so she came across the room to his small kitchen area to help him out. In a panic, he turned round and accidentally splashed some of the hot pasta water onto her hand. His immediate reaction was to put cold water on the wound and plant a kiss on her hand to make it better. That small gesture led to everything else that has happened since.

What else can I tell you about Dad? Well, he likes to enjoy a beer at the weekend. He pronounces it in a weird way though: it sounds more like 'Bear' or 'Bur' or somewhere between the two.

My dad is also football mad. He always has been and always will be. He supports Ipswich Town, who play in blue at Portman Road.

His favourite team win some games but lose just as many. He always sticks by their side, though. I think that's part of why he is a football fan. It would be boring if your team just won every single game, wouldn't it? Because my dad supports Ipswich, it means that they are also my favourite team.

Dad and I used to go to football games together occasionally; despite not loving football myself, it was always nice spending this time with him. I bet Dad was happy I didn't decide to support a team who play a long way from Ipswich, like Glasgow Rangers or Plymouth. It would have been very expensive to take me all the way there to watch the games!

When I was younger, I used to watch Ipswich a lot in the stadiums, but the games often became overwhelming for me. When I started to experience this feeling, Dad would give me a pair of headphones to put over my ears and I would play some of my favourite songs.

Listening to familiar music has a calming

effect, especially in busy situations. Music has the ability to calm me down and make me feel less anxious. It is like the soft music that I usually have playing in my bedroom.

I guess in a way, music is its own superpower, and the best thing is that it can often be found for a low cost and is available to everyone, wherever you are in the world.

Sometimes you will hear a song play and suddenly it opens a memory out of nowhere, sometimes a memory that you haven't thought about for some years. Music has the power to evoke strong emotions. It can take us back to specific times and places in our lives and bring back the feelings associated with those days. I think this is because music is closely tied to our emotional experiences and often used to mark important events in our lifetimes.

Our brains are very open to music, and we can easily remember melodies and lyrics. This is why it is common to get a song stuck in your head or to be able to sing along to a song that you haven't heard for years! Music can bring us comfort, joy, or sometimes it can even bring us to tears. It has the ability to transport the mind, it has the ability to console us, and it has the ability to make tricky situations better. My dad knew all of this so always carried my headphones around with us.

My dad is the world's best dad. You may think I am biased, but it's true. At football, he would often miss part of the game to make sure that I was okay. He wouldn't take his eyes off the game for much longer than thirty seconds though. What if he missed a goal? (Yes, even Ipswich scored goals!). I have been told that my dad has his own superpower, and that is the ability to be very understanding. I couldn't agree more with this.

Another example of Dad's kindness was on my sixteenth birthday. Sixteen is a weird birthday to get excited about. You're getting closer to eighteen, and certainly have so much more independence than when you are two years younger at fourteen. One of the things that excited me when I turned sixteen was that I was finally allowed to buy myself a scratch card! He took me to the shop to get one. He has always been supportive like that. I didn't win though.

Dad would sit in the front row of every school performance I did. I remember looking out from the stage one day to see him in the front row with a bucket of popcorn. It almost made me forget my lines.

He also looked over the homework I had been given for Science or Maths, and tell me that I was tremendously intelligent, even at times when I didn't really feel that way.

Back in 2010, there was a day when he had set up a special superpower for me. The blue bucket was brought in, and I could pick a new superpower for the day. On this day, I pulled out a slip, unfolded it, and took it in. I had been given strength! My favourite superpower!

He must have got my hint about wanting to be strong on that day when I was flying on the ironing board.

Dad knew I was going to pick this out as,

within minutes, he had come into the room, and seemed really eager for me to open the big present he was holding.

"What is it?" I asked, looking at him confused.

He grinned at me, more excited than I had seen him before. "Open it and see."

It looked like he had been waiting weeks to see my face on this day. I tore off the red birthday wrapping paper and found a large square box underneath.

I tore at the sticky tape holding it together, pulled apart the tissue paper inside and lifted out a pair of giant arms. They were like the arms of The Hulk and went up to my elbows. Huge forearms! They weren't green though. Phew, I hate green! Instead, they were red.

I slipped them over my arms and ran immediately to the large square mirror in our front room to check myself out. I looked just like a bodybuilder. I wanted to start hitting things straight away, but Dad had another surprise for me.

"Go to your room, and come down again in about ten minutes," he said.

I did as I was told. When I was in my bedroom, I sat there tapping against the walls gently. I could hear a lot of noise downstairs, but I had no idea what he was up to. I think he had got my mum and sister to help him as well. I stood just behind my door, ready to burst out as soon as I got the signal.

"Bradley, come down!" my mum shouted from the bottom of the stairs. I flew out of my room and bounded down the stairs two at a time, which is difficult when you have massive arms. "Steady, steady," she added as I reached the hallway.

Mum opened the door to the front room and nodded at me to head inside.

Instead of the usual empty space between the sofas, there was a large fake brick wall. It looked like it had been made from shoeboxes, and each had been wrapped in a beige coloured paper with some pen marks on so that they resembled large bricks. These had then been stacked in the middle of the room, just like Jenga!

I wanted to head across and smash it down straight away, before rebuilding it and doing it all over again. Before I was allowed to do so, I had to wait for Emily to play a song on the CD player.

After a couple of false starts on the wrong track, she hit play. It was one of my favourite songs (*'Eye of the Tiger'* - perfect!). I flew across to the pile of bricks and got to work.

ROAAAAARRRR!!!!

I didn't care that they were not real bricks. As you know, I tried punching walls before and it didn't go well. But now? I had superhuman strength and I had no trouble at all destroying this gigantic tower.

The look on my dad's face was priceless. He had been planning this for so long, and you could see how proud he was of me. I was just as proud of him as well.

As I say, he is understanding. He knows exactly how I am feeling all of the time. He knows to give me space if I need it. He knows when to comfort me too. He knows exactly what I need to make things better and will go well out of his way to give that to me. I have heard from so many other people that he has treated them the same way. Best. Dad. Ever!

One funny quirk that Dad has is that when he leaves the room, he will do this weird funny little 'dad wave'. It's quite hard to describe.

Imagine keeping your palm facing forward, and then waggling just a few fingers at a time. It's like that, and he has done it for as long as I can remember. It makes me laugh every time. I bring this up now because once I have my superpower, Dad knows when to do his little wave and leave me alone.

Once I was alone with my strength superpower, I allowed my imagination to take the lead. One moment I was standing on top of a large building in Tokyo, then New York. Alien spaceships were flying at me from all angles, with each trying to attack the Lego people below. From my position on top of the building, I could reach out and hit the spaceships with my strength, and they would fly out of Earth's atmosphere. Then, I would take on zombie armies. I would run at them and spin my arms around like a giant windmill, hitting each of the attackers and destroying them!

I preferred playing by myself. Even to this day, despite no longer being a child, when I am alone, my imagination shines more. You have no limits in what you can do or where you can go in your imagination. When you are alone, no one can get in the middle of your mind and thoughts, no one can judge what you are imagining and tell you that you are doing it wrong.

I used to sit with my imagination for hours, especially when it was a superpower day. Home is a protected space, so I would feel safe to imagine anything that I wanted. Just like playing with my huge, strong arms that day.

But, unfortunately, I didn't feel safe in many places. For example, I didn't feel comfortable at school. When I was at school people often laughed at me. They used to tell me that "my superpowers aren't real".

One morning before I went to school, I was told by my mum that my powers didn't work there. I didn't understand, but she told me that it "was for the best."

It took me time to get used to not being able to experiment with my special superpowers at school. I used to sit alone quite a lot, especially when eating lunch. Most of the time I didn't mind because I had my imagination to keep my company. Other times, I was happy when one of my friends would come sit and chat with me over lunch, even if I couldn't show them my Superpower of the Day.

Sometimes Mysterious

As much as I hated to admit it, not all of my superpowers had been brilliant. My parents always tried their best though, which is important to remember. Initially, it was disappointing to have a superpower that did not live up to my expectations or one that caused more problems than it solved.

I learnt there were ways of coping with this though:

1. Acceptance: first, it's important to accept that a certain superpower may not be what I

wanted or what I thought it would be. This can be tough but it's a necessary step in moving forward.

2. Altering my perspective: instead of focusing on the negatives of the superpower, I always tried to look at the positive aspects. When I was given a superpower that allowed me to have the fastest vehicle, I kept getting motion sickness when I ran around in my cardboard car. That might not seem great but if I focussed on the freedom that it provided, I made the best out of the situation. This goes for most things in life, although it is hard to always view everything in a positive light.

3. Find ways to use my superpower for good: even if my superpower was not as impressive or convenient as I had hoped, I tried to still use it to make a positive impact in my own world. You need to think about how you can use your unique abilities to help others and make a difference.

I think the worst superpower that I was given was the one I had in the beginning of October 2010. On that day, both my parents had to work early, so I knew before even diving into my superpower bucket that it may not have been the most exciting one. The superpower I was given that day was shrinking. By the time I had opened it, my dad had already left for work. There was a note attached to the outside of my bedroom door telling me that there was an item I might find useful in the cupboard under the stairs.

Still in my pyjamas, I made my way downstairs and opened the door. There was a large cardboard box. As I approached, I noticed a sticky note attached to the front of it. It said *"THIS CAN HELP YOU SHRINK"* with a smiley face drawn next to it.

I headed into the utility room and picked up a blanket and a torch; I went to sit in my box. I climbed inside and put the blanket over my head, shutting out all the natural light that was coming through the windows. I turned on the yellow glow of the torch and imagined myself shrinking. When I thought hard, it did seem like I was getting smaller and smaller. I felt so tiny. It felt like I could hide in a small gap between the skirting boards like I was

Jerry the Mouse, hiding from Tom the Cat as he stalked the house.

No one disturbed me in my miniature world. I hoped that I would become so small that I would be able to walk inside all my Lego sets. I could sit in the plane at the Lego airport! I sat in the box, fully covered, for thirty-six minutes.

By this point my legs were starting to ache a little, so I decided to have a little walk before taking my new base upstairs. I went back into my bedroom and opened the wardrobe with plans to camp out in there. I moved some of my belongings out of the way but realised that there were far too many games and toys at the bottom. There wasn't enough room! In the end, I decided to use the wardrobe in my sister's room, which was just next door to mine. I crept along the landing before opening her bedroom door gently and peering inside. I needed to make sure that my sister wasn't there.

I heard her voice travel from downstairs; she was talking to my mum in the kitchen. At the time though, that didn't really matter, because if she was in there, I was so small that I could pass by unnoticed!

As the room was empty, I carried my box inside and opened her wardrobe. My sister didn't have a lot of Lego like me, and her wardrobe was full of clothing. Perfect! I put my box in the bottom and stepped into it, being careful not to knock any of her skirts or tops from their hangers. This was my new little mouse home.

With the blanket over my shoulders and the torch on, I was back in my imagination. I could even hear Tom creeping around the bedroom saying, "I think I can smell Jerry."

I kept still and made sure I made no noise at all. Even my breathing was slow and gentle. I didn't want to be discovered.

Suddenly, the noise got louder. I came back to reality and jumped when I noticed that the noise was real. Someone was nearby! I leant out the box and pushed the wardrobe door gently. I opened it just enough to see across the bedroom.

Emily's bedroom was very neutral in colour. The walls were a nice shade of blue. In the corner of her room was a small desk which had a few books on it, as well as make-up and a pile of magazines. She was much more organised than me, hence why her wardrobe wasn't full of clutter! Her room was always neat and tidy, and it even had a nice smell.

But there she was! My sister was there. She had come upstairs and was lying down on her bed.

I haven't told you about my older sister Emily yet, have I? Emily was born on the twenty-fourth of March 1999, which makes her an Aries (The Ram). Around the time that she was born, a film called The Matrix premiered. I haven't seen the film but the characters in it also have some kind of superpower!

Emily is strong; she has always been very fit and is obsessed with the gym. She is also very protective of me. A few years ago, she threw a whole milkshake over a guy who was being homophobic toward me. I didn't understand the word he had used at the time, so I Googled it when I got home. I knew it wasn't nice, and that Emily had stood up for me.

My sister isn't only strong physically either. Her superpower is that she is constantly strong minded also. For example, she is not afraid to speak her mind when someone says something she disagrees with, even if that person is just speaking on the television or radio.

Despite all the above, there are times when I have noticed her exterior strength crack. One of the first times was when I was sitting in her wardrobe that day. She had entered the room and I knew that something was off. From my viewpoint through the small gap in the door I could see that she was crying.

It wasn't just gentle crying either. She was bawling her eyes out. Literal, full on, one hundred percent sobbing. Obviously, I had no idea why she was crying, but I knew they weren't happy tears. That much was certain.

I had never seen her cry before. I'm not saying that I think she had never cried before this day, that would be silly; it's just that maybe she only ever cried when she thought no one could see. Was she worried that it would make her look vulnerable?

I had two options. Stay in the wardrobe or make myself known. I made a quick mental list of the positives and negatives of each.

Staying in the wardrobe

Positives:

1. It allows Emily to cry in peace.

2. Doesn't scare her.

Negatives:

1. She might come to get some clothes and I scare her.

2. I might sneeze and give the game away.

3. What if Emily stayed for ages. I would be trapped all day (and night!).

Coming out of the wardrobe:

Positives:

1. I could comfort her.

2. It would be less awkward, maybe.

Negatives:

1. If I scare her, it might make the crying worse.

2. She will want to know why I was in her room.

3. She might not want to see me.

I weighed up the options. There seemed to be more negatives than positives for both scenarios, but if I was being truly honest, I didn't want to have to spend a whole day stuck inside the wardrobe. If I really was tiny, I could have snuck out no problem at all.

This was another reason why I didn't enjoy this superpower as much as some of the others. Someone had come and interrupted my imagination and now I was just a boy in a box in a wardrobe. I don't think Marvel would make any films about that in a hurry, do you?

I shifted in my box and took a breather before opening the door. I didn't want to frighten her or make her scream. But I tripped on a pair of her shoes and tumbled out the wardrobe. She screamed. Whoops.

I stood as still as a stone statue for a minute and waited for her to calm down. She turned to me and put her arms stiffly by her sides, before asking the obvious.

"Why are you in my room?" she asked, slowly. There was anger in her tone.

"My superpower was the ability to shrink myself, and I needed to find a space where I could be small," I replied, truthfully.

She looked annoyed. "What was wrong with your own wardrobe?"

"Too much Lego in there." I shrugged.

This was about as much of a conversation we had about the whole situation because after this she simply said 'no' to anything I asked.

"Are you okay?"

"No."

"I saw you cry. Is there anything I can do?"

"No."

"Do you need a hug?"

"No."

"Do you want some homemade
lemonade?"

"No."

"Biscuit?"

"No!"

After exhausting my ideas, I realised that she
wasn't giving me many answers and wanted to be
left alone. Being left alone seemed to be a very
'Riches Family' trait. Emily and I both liked being on
our own (for different reasons and maybe when
feeling different emotions). I am not sure if my
parents also like their own company sometimes
too. I have always been so used to seeing them as a
couple that I have never really thought that they
may need their own space sometimes as well.

I left my sister's room, not removing my box
from the wardrobe, and headed downstairs to the
kitchen. I took a seat next to Mum as she was
making a latté with her fancy machine (my dad
bought her it the previous Christmas; she said it

was her favourite thing in the kitchen). I told her that I had seen Emily crying and asked her to tell me the reasons why.

She gently shrugged, before taking hold of my hand. "Sometimes people are sad, but they aren't ready to talk about it," she said to me. "Emily wanted some alone time, I think. I'll check on her soon."

I was still confused.

"Why was she upset?" I asked mum again.

"Bradley," she started, still holding my hand, "when you get older, you start to experience new and different things, and that can be hard."

This statement didn't do much to reassure me. My mind swirled around like one of those Spin to Win wheel-type prize games you see at school fetes and festivals.

When my thoughts settled, the arrow was telling me that I wasn't being a good brother. I thought that I should have been there for her. I left the table and went back upstairs. I tapped on my sister's door and opened it without waiting for a response. She was sitting on the side of her bed, pulling at a tissue. Her eyes were red, but the tears had slowed. I went across and sat right beside her.

"Hey, Emily," I said. "You are amazing. I think so, anyway. I just wanted to check to see if you are okay. I know you're upset, and I haven't seen you cry before. I couldn't leave you alone in here, knowing that you are sad."

Emily threw her tissue towards the small, beige bin in the corner of her room (but missed), and then turned to give me a hug. As soon as her arms were around me, I shrugged her away and shifted along the bed a bit away from her. I hate people touching my shoulders.

I then thought: 'No Bradley, she needs you'. I moved back closer and hugged her. I embraced her so hard, more than I had ever done, and she started crying onto me. We sat still for around five minutes.

Her breathing calmed; the tears slowed. She sat up and took my hand, just like Mum had done downstairs a few moments previously.

Emily looked me in the eyes and didn't blink

as she said her next words.

"Bradley. I am so proud to call you my brother, even if you are a bit weird and sometimes mysterious, like, y'know, hiding in a box in my wardrobe. But that's you, and I guess that is part of your superpower."

This was the first time that my sister said anything about my superpower. I never realised that she knew I had a real one! She must have noticed this because she told me that I had a puzzled look on my face.

"Don't worry," she then said. "When you find out, the world will make sense. All will be revealed when the time is right."

She tapped my nose and I smiled at her. "Thank you for checking on me," she added.

We spoke a little more before I pulled the box from her wardrobe and returned to my own bedroom. At first, at this age, I thought about changing her superpower as I began to think that she can't be strong minded if she cries. But overtime I realised that this was far from accurate.

Crying doesn't make you a weak person. If anything, it makes you even stronger. Crying is natural. Crying is a way for a person to express their emotions. In fact, crying is a sign of strength and of courage. It shows vulnerability but allows you to feel and express difficult emotions. It is okay to cry, and it is important to allow yourself to cry. It doesn't matter how old you are, what gender you are, where you are from or whatever building blocks have been put together to make you. We all deserve to be able to express our emotions, whether they be sad or happy or somewhere in between.

After seeing my sister cry for the first time, it made me feel something. It was an emotion I'd never felt before and not one that I recognised. It was a bit like suffocation. No, not suffocation. A bear hug? That sounds better. It was like someone had come into my room and wrapped their arms tightly around my middle. It was like someone squeezing my belly so much that I didn't know quite what I was supposed to do. Part of me felt like

I was going to get upset and cry myself, but another part of me was happy that my sister opened up to me.

I sat on my bed, leaning back, and looking at the fairy lights. The soft music was playing. My 'shrinking' box was next to me, and it suddenly looked large now. It seemed to have lost its magical powers after I had seen my sister, and it was now just a cardboard box again.

Was I losing my imagination? I really hoped that I wasn't. I suddenly felt lost and began to cry. It just made me so confused: why was someone as strong as my sister feeling so sad? Why was she so upset that she would rather sit in her room alone? Why didn't she go downstairs and seek comfort from our mum? Why didn't she come to me? She may think I can be weird, but I would have sat with her.

I hoped that my sister's superpower would be strong enough to overcome any sadness that came her way. I knew everyone felt a little sad sometimes, my mum and dad had told me so. When

I was having a bad day or became overwhelmed, they would tell me it's okay, that everyone can get that way sometimes. You just have to be strong and let it pass. You just have to do things that make you happy.

I would make sure that I was there to help her fight her sadness just like when I had my strength, fighting off the aliens across the city. I would stand on the imaginary building with my sister, using my strength to punch away any sad thoughts she had! After all, we are family and family sticks together. They help each other stay happy and find their way through sad times. Mum and Dad had told me this many times. I would do everything I could to help her going forward. I edited my daily routine. At 8.15am every morning I would make sure that she was okay.

Discovery

We are now back in my childhood bedroom. I am writing to you whilst sitting on the floor, my back propped against the wall. I have brought you here to tell you the final part of how I discovered my superpower. I've poured myself a drink (lemonade, obviously) as I'm so thirsty after telling you everything up to here! You can't function fully if you are thirsty, can you?

I am sat against this wall in the exact same position that I had done after speaking to Emily when she had cried, all those years ago. I have been through so much in this bedroom since then. I've laughed in here, cried in here; I've read stories in here, built Lego in here and lost (and found) myself in here my entire life. I do enjoy alone time, but I am glad that you are here with me now.

I look across to the middle of the room at the bucket from which I used to pick my superpowers from. It looks exactly the same as it did years ago when my parents first gave it to me.

Music is playing and I have turned on my rainbow lights. I close my eyes and steady my breathing. I picture myself walking across the room and stepping into the bucket. When I open my eyes, it is the eleventh of December 2010.

∞

The alarm sounds a little bit muffled this morning because I have woken up completely underneath my duvet. It was cold last night, which I guess is expected when it is the middle of December. On the news yesterday evening the weather forecaster said it would be zero degrees overnight so I must have subconsciously buried myself in the warm, like an animal who is hibernating for winter.

Today is obviously an exciting day. Every birthday is. I feel quite grown up now that I am finally nine years old. Last night our whole family sat in front of the television watching a Christmas film. Mum had cooked us all pizza (without any grass on) and it felt like our family was as cosy as the one we were watching on the television. It was perfect.

My sister had gone to her room shortly after the film had finished, but I stayed downstairs with my parents for a bit. I was singing a song from *The Little Shop of Horrors* to them. They love it when I perform musical theatre songs for them! If I could grow up to play any role in any musical, I think it would have to be Seymour from that musical. I have always wanted to be able to play that part! It is such a fun and silly musical, so what is there not to like about it?

One day when I am older, I will be on stage singing and dancing as Seymour... or maybe I might be on television. I cannot wait to see my parent's faces as they watch me do these things, knowing that I am living out my dream, the dream that was being played out in their own front room.

Due to my good mood, I wasn't told to go to bed on time like usual, but when I had tired myself out, I said goodnight and went upstairs. I could hear music playing from Emily's room, so I knocked and opened the door. She was sitting on the bed, reading a magazine.

I had kept up my promise to check on her each day and to make sure she wasn't down. I think we have become a lot closer because of this. She doesn't tell me to get out of her room anymore which is nice. I decided to sit with her for a few minutes.

"What are you reading?" I asked.

"Just some articles," she replied, waving the magazine in my general direction. "I've read most of it already though, so I'll get a new one over the weekend."

I made a note to buy her a magazine if I received any money for my birthday in the morning. With my birthday falling on a Saturday, I wouldn't have to wait for school to finish before I could spend my money this year.

"Are you excited for your birthday?" she had asked me. I nodded back excitedly. "Any idea what you are going to get?"

"No, but Mum and Dad said that I am going to get another superpower," I replied, smiling.

Once I had said this, she put the magazine to one side and went to take hold of my hands.

"Tomorrow's 'Superpower of the Day' is an exciting one!"

"What is it?" I asked.

"All will be revealed tomorrow." She tapped her nose, telling me it's a secret.

Emily is good at keeping secrets, but I know her well enough to understand when she is hiding something extra exciting. I didn't question her more because I knew she wouldn't tell. Maybe when I pick out my superpower tomorrow at 10am, it will be my real superpower. That made me even more excited!

I told Emily to make sure that she is there to

see what I get, even if she did already know. We said goodnight and I went into my room. As I was departing, her eyes followed me out, knowingly.

As I tried to go to sleep that night, Emily's words were playing over and over in my head. It was as if there was something magical attached to every single letter of the sentence.

"All will be revealed tomorrow... ALL. WILL. BE. REVEALED. TOMORROW."

No one has ever said this to me on my birthday-eve before, and I kept thinking about what makes this year different.

∞

8.11am. *DING DING DING*

I turn off my alarm and get out of bed. Looking in the mirror, I notice that I am the same Bradley as the one who went to sleep last night. No giant Hulk arms. A normal sized body, so I haven't shrunk. No wings to allow me to fly. I put on my blue dressing gown and walk towards the bathroom. On the way, I look into my sisters' room, poking my head through the door quietly, but she is still half asleep by the looks of things. I will wake her up before we have breakfast though. She needs to be there when I open my presents. It wouldn't be the same otherwise.

"Morning beautiful," says my mum as she comes out of her bedroom. She kisses me on the forehead, "Happy birthday. The big number nine!"

"Thanks, Mum," I reply happily. I sit on the floor of the landing looking into the bathroom whilst mum makes sure that the water temperature is perfect. Right handle towards six o'clock. Left handle towards three o'clock. I wait until she removes her hand from the shower.

"All yours," she says as she passes by me and goes downstairs.

As I get myself clean, I still can't get Emily's words out of my head. I put a blob of shampoo into my right hand and lather it through my hair. It smells like mint. Suddenly everything hits me all at once. My eyes open wide.

"All will be revealed tomorrow."

My superpower. My real-life superpower.

Tomorrow *is today*! I will find out my real superpower *today*!

No made-up ones from Mum or Dad. Maybe with this one I will be allowed to show it off at school too!

The rest of my shower is rushed. Life will make more sense for me in less than two hours, and I need to get to that moment as quickly as possible. I go back to my bedroom, change into a black shirt and pull a white knitwear tank top over the top. I can't believe after waiting for nine whole years, today is the day that my life will change.

I go to a basket that is stuffed under my bed. Here, there are various props and outfits from my theatre adventures at school. I start pulling out everything, flinging each incorrect item to one side.

It must be in here somewhere. I definitely wouldn't have thrown it away. I reach the bottom, but it isn't there.

"Keep calm, Bradley," I tell myself. I switch on my lights and music. When I go back to the basket, I sit with my legs crossed in front of it. I carefully take each discarded item and start putting them back neatly. This way I will not miss what I am looking for.

I put a few wigs in first. They're hard to fold so I keep them at the bottom to stop bits of hair poking out of the top once it's closed. There are some blue and white chequered trousers. I can't remember what they were from. I put my crown from the nativity back into the box and then I fold about half a dozen t-shirts.

Then I spot it. On top of the pile is my turquoise cape! I wore this in a school production two years ago. If I am going to become a real superhero today, then I need to be wearing my cape.

I think I want my real superpower to be something useful. I put the cape around my shoulders and take the small chalkboard off the top of my bedside table and write MY POWER across the top in big letters. I then take a piece of yellow chalk and start a list of what I might want it to be:

The power to heal anyone.

With this I would be able to tell straight away if someone was feeling sad or low and know exactly what I would need to do to make things better for them. I would love to be able to help Emily.

Strength

I've already technically had this, and that was great fun. Would I want it for life though? I am still unsure.

Invisibility

I could use this to secretly check on things. Or to sneak into places. Actually, I am not sure I would want this one. I take a damp cloth and scrub invisibility from the chalkboard.

Superspeed!

I would love to be as fast as lightning again, like Dash from *The Incredibles*! It would mean that I could run anywhere and back (even to Tesco Express) in 0.011 seconds. Now that would be cool.

I've already said how *The Incredibles* is my favourite film. I used to have a copy of the poster on my bedroom wall. Yes, this is an exciting power. I sing the theme tune in my head as I write on my board.

Time Travel

Is this a superpower or is it more scientific? I'll allow it for now. If I had the choice to travel to any point in time, I think I would travel back to the time when dinosaurs ruled the Earth. I think my favourite dinosaur is the Pterodactyl. I have seen them in films gliding through the sky.

Teleportation

If I had this, I would snap my fingers and wake up in the Canary Islands. These are located just to the north-west of Africa and I have been once before. I loved it there! To be able to go without having to deal with a stressed-filled airport would be magical.

Now, I could write on this chalkboard all day, but I need to have breakfast and open my presents before I find out the answer that I have been waiting for.

I place the chalk down and jump down the stairs really fast until I reach the kitchen. There are several presents in square boxes stacked neatly on the table. Mum has poured me a glass of lemonade; I sit down and open my cards.

There is a nice one from my parents and Emily. They have got me a Pixar card which even has a big number 9 badge attached to the front. Dad helps me pin it to my tank top so that I don't hurt myself. I've got cards from some of my friends at school and all the extended family of course. I'm so excited about everything that I drink my lemonade a bit too quickly and give myself hiccups.

I check the clock. 9.35am. Just twenty-five minutes before my life is changed! I start to open the presents. Mum is keeping one near to her so this must be the one that she is most excited for me to open. I get some cool things to play with. I want to take things out of their boxes as soon as I open them, but my parents are doing a good job of keeping the flow of unwrapping going. Emily picks up all the wrapping paper and puts it in the bin.

Finally, the main present is brought across. I move it from side to side, and the rattle of the contents seems so familiar and comforting. I tear at the paper as quickly as I can and pull out a Lego City Police Station! I'm so happy, and I'm pretty sure my mum even has tears in her eyes seeing how pleased I am with it. As it's the weekend, I can build this with Dad straight away!

I have been given another glass of lemonade. I take sips of it whilst staring at the back of the Lego box, imagining all the different games I can play with it. It will work so well with some of my other sets in the wardrobe too. I am so engrossed that I don't notice that the time has ticked along and now there is only one minute to go until I find out my superpower.

Dad comes through holding the magic bucket in his hands and places it in front of me. My parents are hugging each other. They seem a bit nervous, unlike me.

I can't wait.

I put my hand into the box and notice there is only one bit of paper left. I look at my dad who nods to tell me that this is meant to be happening. Emily is biting at the sleeve of her jumper. I take the paper from the bucket and nearly burst with excitement. Finally, it's time to find out my real superpower.

I take the piece of paper, and slowly unroll it in my hands.

I stare at the word in front of me. I don't understand what it means.

I look at my parents, they are smiling, but they still seem nervous.

I want to Google this, just like I always do when I don't understand a word. I run to my bedroom. My parents call after me, but I ignore them for now.

I look at the chalkboard. It isn't the ability to heal, it isn't lightning speed or strength, it's not time travel or even invisibility.

I'm feeling very confused. I sit in the middle of the floor and think about my breathing for a bit. When I feel ready, I read my piece of paper again.

"A...Au...Au...Autism," I stutter, not fully knowing how to say the word.

That is all that is written down.

I need my music, so I switch it on. And my lights. I need my lights! I turn them on. Autism isn't what I was expecting. It was probably the last thing I was expecting because I don't really know what it is.

I turn on my computer and Google it, hoping that somewhere will explain it. The internet tells me that my brain works in a different way from other people. What does that mean? It doesn't mean that I am ill or have a disease. But how does my brain work differently? I sit there confused until I hear my mum and dad coming up the stairs.

When they tap gently on my door, I allow them to come in. Mum sits on the floor next to me but knows not to touch my shoulders. Dad sits on the bed to my right. The glass of lemonade has been placed on my desk so I will drink that when I'm ready. We remain in silence for a few moments.

"Bradley," says my dad finally. I turn to look at him. He adds, "there is something else I want you to read."

He hands me an envelope. I open it and pull out a rainbow-patterned piece of card. I look at the bold, black writing across the middle.

YOU ARE ENOUGH
YOU ARE GIFTED
YOU HAVE A BEAUTIFUL IMAGINATION
FIND YOUR SUPERPOWER AND LET IT
FREE YOU

I am really struggling because I hate the feeling of being uncertain, the feeling of not knowing answers.

I thought it would be a superpower that would stop me feeling confused. This piece of card has given me zero answers! I stand up quickly, which makes my mum jump.

"Bradley," my mum smiles, and it gives me a sense of familiar comfort. Maybe everything isn't changing like I thought it was. "This may seem scary at first, but being autistic doesn't change who you are in here-" Her finger points to my heart.

"If anything, it adds to you and your character," adds my dad. "It makes you stronger, more special, more gifted! It's a superpower that you just have to learn to control."

"And we are here, and will always be here, to help you." My mum leans forward and hugs me. I tense but let her embrace me for a few seconds.

"We don't have to explain everything about autism to you right now but knowing a few things may make you feel more understood. You like routines, don't you?"

I nod.

"Autism is associated with having routines and order, just how you like it. As well as sometimes having trouble communicating and not understanding some social situations. Does any of this relate to you?"

I nod again, but I'm not sure what to say yet. What my parents are saying does make sense to me, and I do see those traits in myself, but just because it explains some of my traits, it doesn't mean it controls who I am or the person I will become through childhood.

"Would you like a break? Some alone time?" Mum asks, patting my arm. He knows me too well.

I nod a third time. "Yes, please."

"We will be back up to see you in ten minutes," she says, as she leads my dad out of the room.

I am feeling overwhelmed, so I decide to do something creative. I pull out my paints from the box under my bed and put an apron around me. Once it is tied, I put on my headphones and start to paint.

I pull out a new A3 canvas to work on. I start by drawing a large rainbow across the top of the board.

Next, I draw my superpower bucket. It is blue, like the real one. I leave a gap in the middle where I can write 'Superpower of the Day' in red paint.

Now the most important part. Me!

I decide to paint myself exactly how I am today. I draw my black sleeves, my white tank top, my turquoise cape, and I even get the parting in my hair perfect!

Painting and music relax me. I have always been creative. Often, people are jealous about how creative I am!

Everyone wants to be in my drama group. I think the reason why people want to be in my group at school is because they say my ideas are always unique.

That's it. Always unique. My mum has often said that I am 'always unique'.

Is part of my superpower always being unique?

I go over to my chalkboard again and rub everything else off, before writing 'always unique' on it.

ALWAYS

UNIQUE

What else am I good at? I have always been awesome at problem solving because I love when there is an answer to something, and I can always work it out.

Once, I was teaching my sister ratios (which are my favourite), and she couldn't really understand it at all, despite me going over it at what I thought was quite a slow pace.

I found ratios very easy. Each time I got the answer right, my dad would say that I am 'tremendously intelligent', just like he always does. Emily sometimes says this too but with a hint of sisterly sarcasm.

ALWAYS

UNIQUE

TREMENDOUSLY

INTELLIGENT

Oh yeah, my sister said that I am sometimes weird and mysterious, like when I jumped out from her wardrobe and my shrinking box. Some say being weird is a bad thing, but I say it's fun. It's interesting and again, unique!

I take a step back. My new painting and my chalkboard are side by side.

ALWAYS

UNIQUE

TREMENDOUSLY

INTELLIGENT

SOMETIMES

MYSTERIOUS

AUTISM

Autism is my superpower! I look back at the rainbow card that Dad gave me, and it all makes sense now.

My superpower means that I have extra special gifts. I am enough. I have an amazing imagination. I am creative. I am unique. My superpower is within me. I just needed to find it and be free.

Well, today I have found it and I have never felt so free.

...and on to today

The day that I found out that I was autistic was many years ago now. We are back in my front room, but I'm now much older. I am also extremely happy. A lot has changed over the years, of course, but I am still always unique, tremendously intelligent, and sometimes mysterious (and weird). I love it.

My family are still very much the same as they were and have been nothing but supportive of whatever it is that I want to do. I never know what to say to people who ask me questions about why I am different. If I told them that it is a superpower, they would likely laugh.

But it is my superpower.

What people might not realise is that it has been my superpower every single day since I was born.

Being autistic isn't "being odd" or "being strange".

Being autistic is waking up at the exact same time every single day.

Being autistic is having a routine that you need to stick to.

Being autistic is making sure that the shower dials are at six and three o'clock.

Being autistic is about not liking grass on pizza.

Being autistic is being sad and anxious about the texture of your socks.

Being autistic is hating having to wear the top you just had your hair cut in.

Being autistic is arriving somewhere three hours early so that you aren't late.

Being autistic is playing by yourself.

Being autistic is separating your food into sections.

Being autistic is not looking people directly in the eye when talking to them.

Being autistic is loving your special interests.

Being autistic is being creative and feeling overwhelmed at the same time.

Being autistic is having an incredible imagination.

Being autistic is about you being always unique.

Being autistic is about you being tremendously intelligent.

Being autistic is about you being sometimes mysterious.

Being autistic is being yourself in the most incredible way possible.

Being autistic is all of this and more.

Being autistic is beautiful.

And the best thing is that it is different for everyone.

∞

Today I am packing my magic bucket away for the final time. My bucket that gave me so much freedom, and the opportunity to be myself. My bucket taught me vital and valuable lessons about myself that any class at school couldn't teach me.

I hope that this bucket has helped someone that has now heard my story. I hope it has made you realise that you aren't strange. You are beautiful and unique.

My real superpower has more strength and more resilience than any other superpower that I took from my magic bucket.

As a reminder of my journey, I kept the painting of me and my superpower bucket that I created on my ninth birthday.

I would love for you to see it one day.

Acknowledgements

Bradley Riches

Where do I begin?

My first thanks goes out to James A Lyons for putting down all my ideas, and using his creative mind to come up with new ideas, and put them down into the book so eloquently. I couldn't have done this amazing project without him!

My second thanks goes out to the amazing Illustrator Katie. We had many mutual friends, yet our paths never crossed until this moment. That Instagram DM asking them to come on board was the best idea ever! They created the cover with love and passion, as well as bringing all mine and James's words to life through art! Thank you so much Katie x

My next thanks goes out to Chloe D'Inverno who edited the book and did such an incredible job in making sure it was the best it could be! Thank you for being a part of the team, and I'm so excited to see your future work!

I would also love to say thanks to Corinna Brown and Scott Johnston, who did an incredible job on the audiobook, bringing the characters to life! As well as Scott who produced the audio book!

I would also like to say thanks to my family! My sister, my dad, and my mum, who let me see the beauty in being autistic. They taught me that being different is something to be proud of, and without them I wouldn't be able to be proud of who I am, as well as accomplishing everything that I have done!

Another thanks goes out to all the young autistic and neurodivergent readers, and to everyone who sees themselves in this story! Your support is amazing. I hope you resonated with the story, and you are proud to be different!

My final thanks goes out to younger me! Thank you for being patient and being strong. Thank you for giving yourself time and space to educate yourself and understand who you are! I'm so proud of you!

Love Bradley x

James A Lyons

Firstly, thank you to Bradley for allowing me to work on your story. I am so proud of what we have achieved with this, from the moment you first sent the playscript, right up until now as we prepare to allow everyone to see it. I have learnt so much during the process, and I know this book will be so important to young autistic and neurodivergent people.

This book wouldn't be this book without Katie. The way that you took my rambling emails about what we needed and turned them into such perfect illustrations is amazing! Thank you also to Chloe for your editing skills and adding new depth and perspective to the story.

Thanks also to David for reading over bits as I was writing and making sure they made sense,

A huge thanks to absolutely anyone who has supported this book, whether that is by pre-ordering of buying a copy, buying a ticket to our signings, or even just spreading the word on social media. It really means a lot, and we genuinely couldn't have got this project to where it is now without your support. A special mention here to Fran, who has been like a one person PR machine these last few months. Who knows, one day I might even understand TikTok live, but don't hold your breath.

Finally, thank you to all my family and friends in Witney, Bournemouth and beyond who always tell me that I can at the times when I say that I can't.

Big love,

James x

Support & Advice

National Autistic Society – www.autism.org.uk

The National Autistic Society aim to transform lives by providing support, information, and practical advice for more than 700,000 autistic adults and children in the UK, as well as their three million family members and carers. They also aim to change attitudes by improving public understanding of autism and helping businesses, local authorities, and government to provide more autism-friendly spaces, deliver better services and improve laws.

Ambitious About Autism - www.ambitiousaboutautism.org.uk

Ambitious About Autism stand with autistic children and young people, championing their rights and creating opportunities. They run specialist education services, an award-winning employment programme and children and young people are at the heart of the charity's decision-making, policy work and campaigning. They also use expertise to deliver training and consultancy to a wide range of organisations to improve awareness and understanding of autism.

Autism Aware UK - https://www.autismaware.co.uk/

Autism Aware UK (AAUK) work hard to raise awareness of autism spectrum disorder (ASD). AAUK offers support to families affected by autism by sharing information and offering advice or just being there to listen. AAUK also donates specialist equipment to schools and groups that support/educate people with ASD.

Autism Together - www.autismtogether.co.uk

For over 50 years, Autism Together has been providing support to people on the autism spectrum, offering a wide range of residential services, supported living, day services and community support. Autism affects everyone differently, so Autism Together work with each individual to help them overcome the difficulties the condition presents them with, helping them to lead a creative and fulfilling life.

BeyondAutism - www.beyondautism.org.uk

Their vision is to ensure autistic children and young adults access an education which empowers a life full of choice, independence, and opportunity.

Child Autism UK - www.childautism.org.uk

Child Autism UK helps children with autism achieve their potential. They provide services to enable children to overcome difficulties with communication, learning and life skills and give families the techniques and strategies to cope with autism through the use of Applied Behaviour Analysis (ABA). Child Autism UK also provides training and a network for ABA professionals working with young children.

Printed in Great Britain
by Amazon

32191607R00059